T0105184

I am so 3 !

Sky Pony Press books may be purchased in bulk at special discounts for sales promotion, corporate gifts, fund-raising, or educational purposes. Special editions can also be created to specifications. For details, contact the Special Sales Department, Sky Pony Press, 307 West 36th Street, 11th Floor, New York, NY 10018 or info@skyhorsepublishing.com.

Sky Pony® is a registered trademark of Skyhorse Publishing, Inc.®, a Delaware corporation.

Visit our website at www.skyponypress.com.

Authors, books, and more at SkyPonyPressBlog.com.

10 9 8 7 6 5 4 3 2 1

Library of Congress Cataloging-in-Publication Data is available on file.

Cover design and illustration by John Kurtz

Print ISBN: 978-1-5107-4510-0
Ebook ISBN: 978-1-5107-4513-1

Printed in China

I am so 3!

LOOK AT EVERYTHING I CAN DO!

Sandrina and John Kurtz

Sky Pony Press
New York, New York

I can say,
"Nice to
meet you,"

**and "Happy Birthday"
with a card.**

I can blow bubbles,

and learn to swim.

I can sweep
the patio,

and wash the car.

I can draw pictures,

and make paintings.

I can brush my dog,

and feed my cat.

I can
look at books,

and play in sprinklers.

I can ride a pedal car,

and balance on
one foot.

I can put my own socks on,

and pour drinks.

I can help in the kitchen,

and set the table.

I can act
in a play,

and sing songs.

I can play
hide and seek,

and toss a ball.

I can plant flowers,

and water them.

I can bowl,

and climb
up a hill.

I can sculpt with play dough,

and do a puzzle.

With music and my drum
I'm happy as can be.
I can do all these things
because I am so three!